Carbery's practical work on coat cutting

James Joseph. [from old catalog] Carbery

Very respectfully yours,

James J. Carbery.

CARBERY'S

Practical Work on Coat Cutting,

. . . . WITH . . . .

Diagrams and Full Instructions How to Use Them.

. . . ALSO . . .

A COMPLETE HISTORY OF THE SYSTEM.

. . . . WITH A . . . .

Concise History of the Origin and Progress of the Art.

THIS WORK CONTAINS THE RELATION OF THE OLD SYSTEMS OF CUTTING TO THE SCIENTIFIC AND PRACTICAL EXPERIENCE OF THE NEW; THE ESTABLISHMENT AND GROWTH OF KNOWLEDGE IN THE ART AND MYSTERY OF CUTTING, ESPECIALLY IN THE UNITED STATES OF AMERICA.

BY

J. J. CARBERY,

THREE RIVERS, MICH.

PRICE, $5.00.

KALAMAZOO, MICHIGAN:
KALAMAZOO PUBLISHING COMPANY,
1896.

PREFACE.

As Gibbon has said, "Every man has two educations—one which he receives from others, and one, more important, which he gives to himself."

Sir Walter Scott says: "The best part of every man's education is that which he gives himself."

The mind has been endowed with no more laudable or profitable ambition than that of self-improvement. The educated cutter carries with him his own capital. The ability to not only fit the form of his client but to impart the grace and style peculiarly his own, is a treasure which every cutter should fully appreciate and strive to possess.

In preparing the present work, the author has endeavored to omit no point that may be useful to the cutter. It is customary to burden the initial pages of a new publication with apologies. The author of this work has none to make. He has invested twenty-four years of the best of his life, together with a great amount of diligent, paintaking labor and research, and recognizes the fact that it must depend upon merit and excellence for its success.

INTRODUCTION.

IT is our good fortune to live in an age whose master-pieces of accomplishments in Science, Industry and Commerce put to shame the extravagant fictions of oriental tales and the wonders ascribed to the gods and heroes of ancient history and mythology. The changes produced by recent investigations and discoveries are so vast and rapid that it is difficult to comprehend the power and the thoroughness of the transformations that are taking place in the world around us. The application of steam and electricity astonish us by their wide-spread influence over the condition and relation of men; the ease and speed of movement and intercourse constantly increasing, are ever putting us in new and unfamiliar situations. We have hardly accustomed our thoughts and habits to one before we are hurried on into another. The constant and abundant light shed by Science, or the press, does not suffice to keep our minds fully up to the progress that goes on in all departments of life.

It is plain that we have entered upon a new era, the most extraordinary and momentous the world has ever seen. The old and imperfect is being cleared away, and everything thoroughly reconstructed. The explanation is that we are now setting up the grand temple of civilization, the separate stones and pillars of which, each nation and age was commissioned to hew, carve, and leave in the quarry awaiting the time when, all the material being ready, the Master Builder should collect all the scattered parts and raise the whole edifice at once, to the astonishment and joy of all mankind.

It is plain that the general mind moving us has grown clearer and more accurate in its judgment as experience has accumulated, and former incongruities are being laid aside, and oversights corrected. Likewise the rapidity of growth in Scientific Coat Cutting is being more clearly revealed every day. Yet more intelligence and more care would have saved us many shocks, and made our success pronounced and more brilliant.

Knowledge is power, when wisely applied, and more intimate acquaintance with more practical and accurate cutting, as well as true measurements, will assist cutters to correct all defects in all the old rules of cutting, and enable them to speedily reach that acme of perfection in practical cutting. I, therefore, urge you to accept the efforts of a practical man, who shall give you the fullest information in all its details.

THE INDENTATION AND HOW TO TAKE MEASURES.

The Indentation Measure at neck is taken by placing a yard-stick perpendicularly between shoulder blades and center of hips; while in this position, measure in from stick to nape of neck.

HOW TO TAKE MEASURES.

LOCATE nape of neck as at 1. Locate 2 with a strip of zinc 18 or 20 inches long and 1½ inches wide, with a spirit level on one end. Place end under arm, and bend the other end across the back, keeping it level, and mark 2 on customer. Then measure half way between 1 and 2, and put a mark for 6. Locate natural waist. Now commence and measure from 1 to 6, to 2, to natural waist, to fashionable waist, and full length of coat. Put long arm of square under arm of customer, with short arm pressed close to back of arm, and make mark at 17, and from 17 to elbow, and continue to wrist bone for length of sleeve. *Place instrument under the arm and in the position represented on diagram. Measure from 8 to 2, blade measure, and from 8 to 3 the ecliptic measure, and from 8, up the front of arm-hole, to nape of neck at B. From 8, up the front of arm-hole over shoulder, to 6; this measure finds the center of shoulder at dot. Now measure from 8, up in front of arm-hole and over shoulder, to 2. This gets the slope of shoulder which locates dot on top of shoulder point. Then take breast measure and also waist measure and top of hip. I never take the scye measure, as I get everything exact without. It can be taken if you wish. The sleeve is cut as explained. The measures for a Frock or Surtout Overcoat, or for a Sack Overcoat, should always be taken over an undercoat.

MEASURES AS TAKEN.

9	Depth of Scye, with addition of ½ inch	9½
17	Natural Waist	17
19	Fashionable Waist	19
33½	Full Length for Cutaway	33½
37½	" " " Prince Albert	37½
29	" " " Single- and Double-Breasted Sack	29
40	" " " Overcoat	40
7	Width of Back, with additions	7½
20½	to Elbow, with additions	21
31	Full Length	31
11¾	Blade Measure, with additions	12¾
12¼	Ecliptic " " "	12⅜
11¾	First Over, ' "	13
13¾	Second Over, " "	15
16½	Third Over, " "	17¾
8¼	Small of Waist, " "	9¼
8¾	Spring for Skirt, " "	9¾
37	Breast Measure	37
34	Waist Measure	34

This will show the necessary additions to be made when measures are taken over vests; these additions will also be added to overcoat measures when taken over undercoats.

---

* The instrument that locates 8, 10 and 11 is made of stiff brass. It is 21 inches long. 6½ inches from top have a short arm 9 inches long, with spirit level on end of it, so as to locate perfectly 10 and 11 on line with 8 on front of scye.

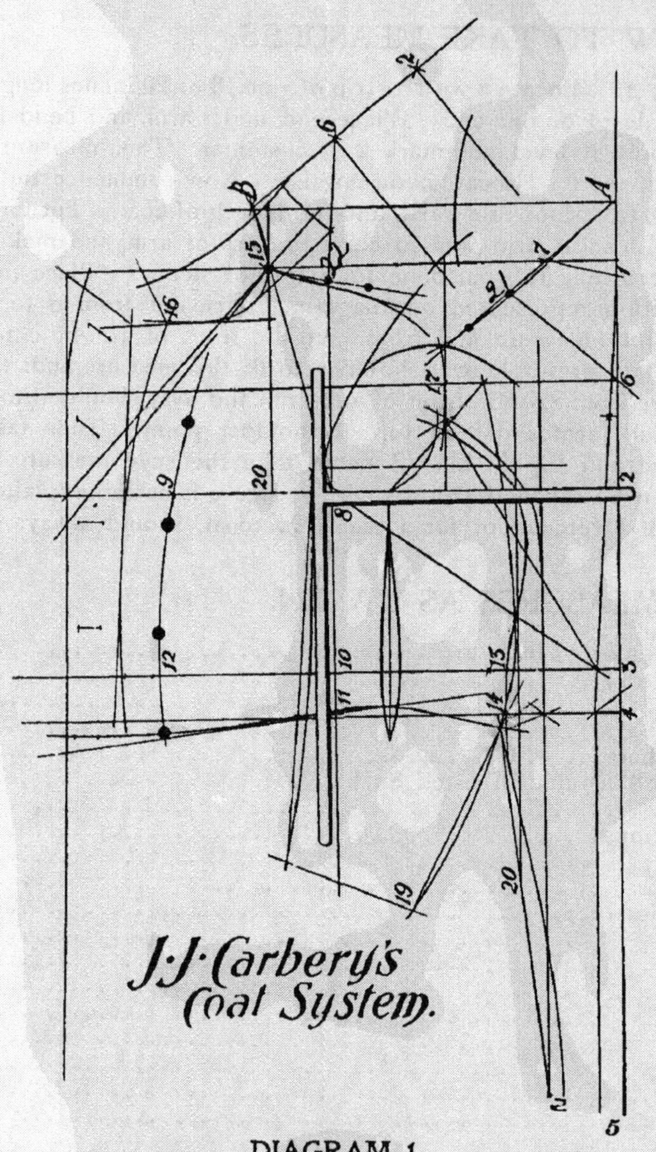

DIAGRAM 1.

PRINCE ALBERT OR DOUBLE-BREASTED FROCK:

DIAGRAM 1.

THE MEASURE, WITH ADDITIONS, ARE:

9	Depth of Scye	9½	12¼	Ecliptic Measure	12⅝
17	Natural Waist	17	11¾	Front Shoulder Measure	13
19	Fashionable Waist	19	13¾	2nd Front Shoulder Measure	15
37½	Full Length	37½	16½	Slope of Shoulder	17¾
7	Width of Back	7	8¼	Small of Waist	9¼
20½	to Elbow	21	8¾	Hip Measure	9¾
31	Full Length of Sleeve	31	37	Breast Measure	37
11¾	Blade Measure	12¾	34	Waist Measure	34

TO DRAFT

COMMENCE by squaring lines A5 and AB. From A to 2 is the front measure taken from 8 to B, with one inch added. From 2 to 1 is depth of scye plus ½ inch. From 1 to 3 is natural waist, 4 is fashionable waist, 5 full length. 6 is half way between 1 and 2. Square lines 1, 6, 2, 3, 4 and 5. Go in one inch at 3 and 5. *From 1 to 7 is ⅛ of half breast measure and ⅜ of an inch added. Go up ¾ of an inch to 7. From 6 to 17 is width of back. Draw line up and down from 17. Go up from 17 1½ inches. Go down from 17 1½ inches. Make width of back at 3 and 4. Shape back as represented. From 2 to 8 is blade measure. From 8 to 3 is ecliptic measure. Whatever the difference is from 8 to 3, take out same between back and side-body on ecliptic line. Measure size of back at 3 and place the amount at 10, and measure back to 13, add 1 inch. Measure back at 4 and place the amount at 11, and measure back to 14; add 1 inch to measure. Draw line from 13 through 14 for spring of skirt. Add a little round on skirt over seat. Now shape back according to style. Now shape back of side-body according to line on ecliptic; take out (under the arm) the difference between small of waist and ecliptic measure. Divide the width of shoulder of back by 3, and place ⅓ the measure in front of 8 at 20. Square up at 20 to 15. From B to 16 is half of shirt-collar measure with ¾ of an inch added. From 2 to 9 is half breast measure. Measure back at 3 and place the amount at 13, and measure half of waist to 12. From 9 to front on breast is 3 inches, and from 12 to front on waist is 2¾ inches. The lapel is 2 inches at bottom, and 2½ inches at breast line, and 2⅛ inches at top. Now measure from 6 to 21, place the amount at bottom of scye at 8, and measure up to 22. This gives the height of shoulder in center. Cut out back. Place 15 and 7 together, 21 and 22 together. Shape shoulder. Shape arm-hole, taking out a little at top of side-body. Shape front of skirt as represented.

THE SLEEVE

THE Sleeve is one of the most important points in coat cutting, and should be drafted with the body of the coat, that it may fit perfectly the coat for which it was intended, and not any and all coats in general.

TO DRAFT SLEEVE

DRAW line in front of arm up and down. Square line 8 and 2. Square line 13-3 from line in front. Go up from 8 1¼ inches and square across. Measure from this point 1¼ inches above 8 up to point of shoulder, and apply this amount to back and measure down to 17. Whatever the measurement is, make that the distance from 1¼ inches above 8 to the back part of sleeve on line 17 and 6. Square down from this point, and shape top of sleeve through shoulder of back and strike line 17 in front of scye and down to top line 1¼ inches above 8. Go out 1-24 of half breast measure at this point, at 8. Go out 1-12 at 10. Draw line from 1-24 through 1-12. Go in 1 inch for under sleeve at back. Measure width of back; apply this to top of sleeve. Measure to 18 at elbow, and to 19 full length. Make sleeve at bottom 12 inches when made up. Hollow the sleeve ½ inch at 10. This is the only sure method of cutting a sleeve and having it fit and look well.

* Draw line from 1 to 3 and from 3 to 5.

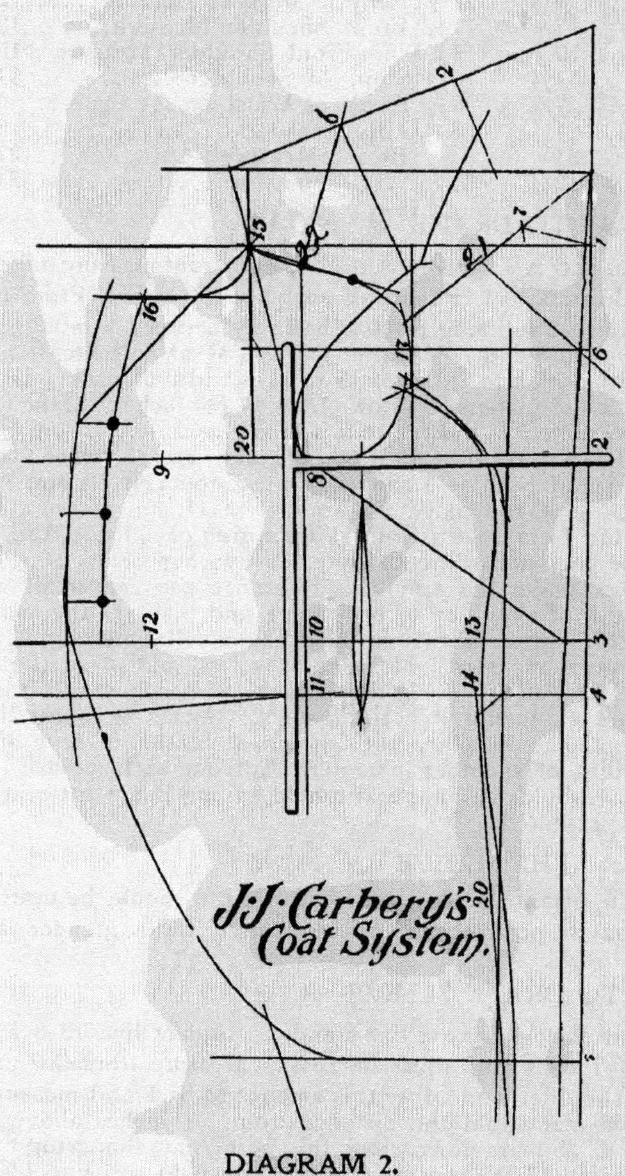

DIAGRAM 2.

CUTAWAY.

DIAGRAM 2.

THE MEASURES, WITH ADDITIONS, ARE:

9	Depth of Scye	9½	12¼	Ecliptic Measure	12⅜
17	Natural Waist	17	11¾	Front Shoulder	13
19	Fashionable Waist	19	13¾	2nd Front Shoulder Measure	15
33½	Full Length	33½	16½	Slope Shoulder	17¾
7	Width of Back	7	8¼	Small of Waist	9¼
20½	to Elbow	21	8¾	Hip Measure	9¾
31	Full Length of Sleeve	31	37	Breast Measure	37
11¾	Blade Measure	12¾	34	Waist Measure	34

TO DRAFT.

SQUARE lines A5 and AB. From A to 2 is the front measure taken from 8 to B, with 1 inch added. From 2 to 1 is actual depth of back scye measure plus ½ inch. From 1 to 3 is natural waist, and to 4 is fashionable waist; 5 is full length. 6 is half way between 1 and 2. Square lines 1, 6, 2, 3, 4 and 5. Go in 1 inch at 3 and also at 5. Draw line from 1 to 3 and from 3 to 5. From 1 to 7 is ⅛ of half breast measure plus ⅜ inch. Go up ¾ inch to 7. From 6 to 17 is width of back. Draw line up and down from 17. Go up from 17 1½ inches. *Make back 2¼ inches wide at 3 and 4, and for all sizes over 45 breast make the back at 3 and 4 3 or 2⅞ inches. Now shape back as represented. From 2 to 8 is blade measure. From 8 to 3 is ecliptic measure. Whatever the difference is from 8 to 3, take out the same amount on the ecliptic line, as represented on draft. Measure size of back at 3 and place the amount at 10 and measure back to 13 plus 1 inch. Measure size of back at 4, place the amount at 11, and measure back to 14; add 1 inch. Draw line from 13 through 14 for spring of skirt. Add a little round over seat in skirt. Now shape back of side-body according to line on ecliptic, and take out, under the arm, the difference between small of waist and ecliptic measure. Divide the width of shoulder of back by 3 and place ⅓ in front of 8 at 20. Square up from 20 to 15. From B to 16 is half the size of shirt collar with ¾ inch added. From 2 to 9 is half breast measure. Add 3½ inches from 9 to front. Measure width of back at 3, placing the amount at 13, and measure to 12, half waist measure; add 3½ inches to front. Measure from 6 to 21, placing the amount at bottom of scye at 8, and measure up to 22 to get height of shoulder in center. Cut out back and place 15 and 7 together and 21 and 22 together. Shape shoulder as represented. Shape arm-hole. Take out ½ inch at top of side-body between top of back. Shape front of skirt as represented on diagram.

* Go down from 17 1½ inches.

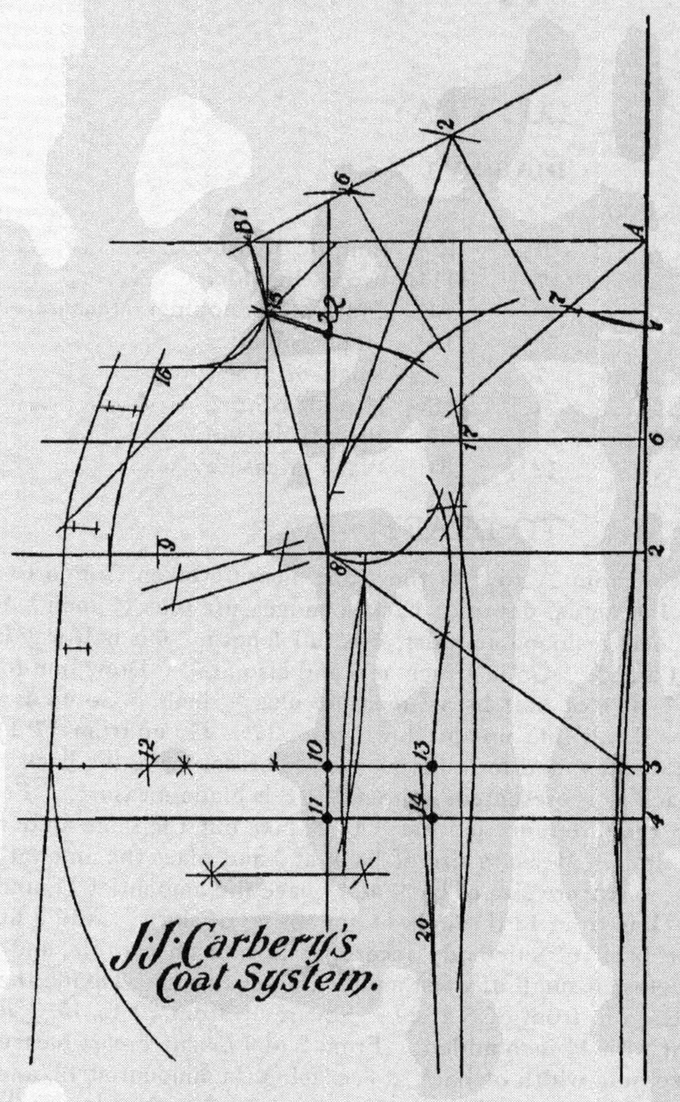

DIAGRAM 3.

SINGLE- AND DOUBLE-BREASTED SACK.

DIAGRAM 3.

THE MEASURES, WITH ADDITIONS, ARE:

9	Depth of Scye	9½	12¼	Ecliptic Measure	12⅜
17	Natural Waist	17	11¾	Front Shoulder Measure	13
19	Fashionable Waist	19	13¾	2d " " "	15
29	Full Length	29	16½	Slope of Shoulder	17¾
7	Width of Back	7½	8¼	Small of Waist	9¼
20½	to Elbow	21	8¾	Hip Measure	9¾
30	Full Length of Sleeve	31	37	Breast Mea-ure	37
11¾	Blade Measure	12¾	34	Waist Measure	34

TO DRAFT.

SQUARE lines A5 and AB. From A to 2 is the front shoulder measure taken from 8 to B with 1 inch added. From 2 to 1 is depth of scye on back plus ½ inch. From 1 to 3 is natural waist; 5, full length of coat; 6 is half way between 1 and 2. Square lines 1, 6, 2, 3, 4 and 5. Go in 1 inch at 3 and 5. Draw lines from 1 to 3 and from 3 to 5. Hollow back at 3 ½ inch. From 1 to 7 is ⅛ and ⅜ of an inch. Go up ¾ of an inch. From 6 to 17 is width of back. Draw line from 17, up and down, to bottom of coat. Go up 1½ inches from 17 for shoulder. Take out a half inch from back at 23. Shape back. From 2 to 8 is blade measure. From 8 to 3 is the ecliptic. Whatever the difference is from 8 to 3, take out on ecliptic line between back and side, as represented. Measure size of back at 3, placing the amount at 10, and measure back to 13. Measure back at 4, placing the amount at 11, and measure back to 14. Add 1 inch to 13 and also to 14. Draw a line from 13 through 14 for spring of hip. Now shape side of fore part according to ecliptic measure through 20 to bottom. Take out, under the arm, the difference between small of waist and ecliptic measure. Divide the width of shoulder of back by 3, and place ⅓ the amount in front of 8 at 20. Square up from 20 to 15. Go down on line 20 ⅛ breast measure and square out to 16. Measure the size of shirt collar to 16 and add ¾ inch. From 2 to 9 is half breast measure, and from 9 to front is 3½ inches. Measure back at 3, placing the amount at 13, and measure out to 12, half waist measure. From 12 to front coat is 3½ inches. For a double-breasted coat there should be added 4¾ inches to breast from 9 to front, and from 12 to front 4¼ inches. Now cut out back and put 15 and 7 together, also 21 and 22. Shape shoulder and arm-hole. Center of shoulder is found the same as on the other drafts.

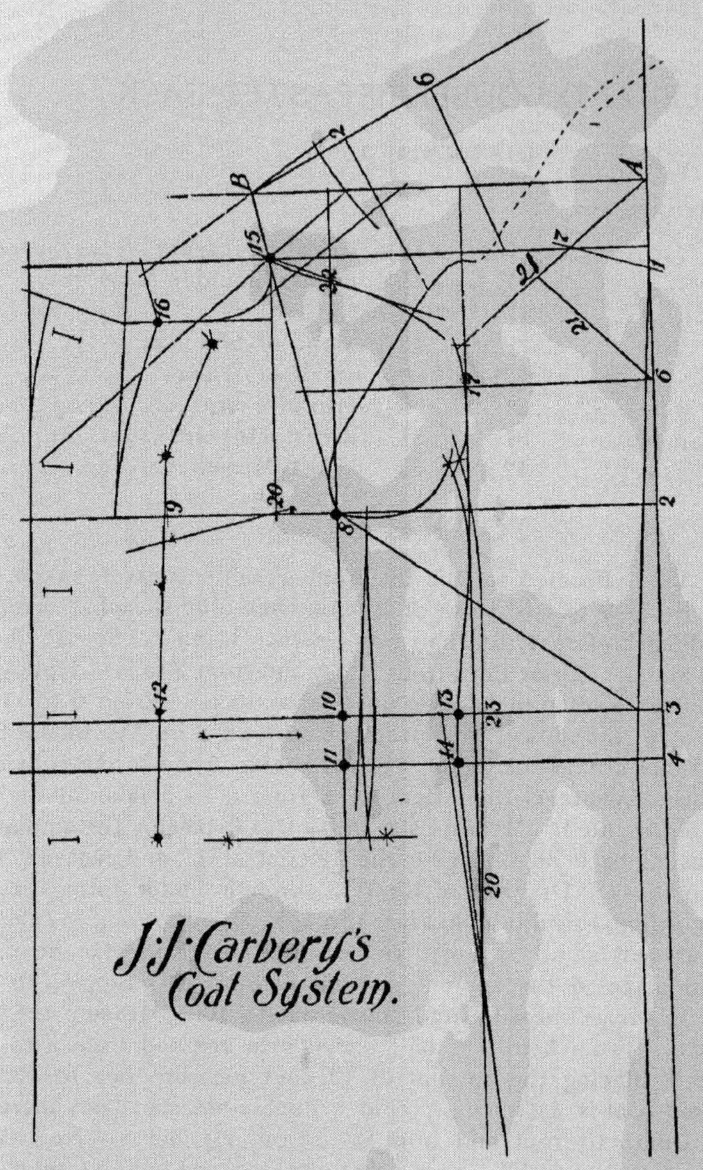

DIAGRAM 4.

OVERCOAT.

Diagram 4.

THE MEASURES, TAKEN OVER THE UNDERCOAT, WITH THEIR ADDITIONS, ARE AS FOLLOWS:

10	Depth of Scye	10¼	13¾	Ecliptic Measure	13¾
17½	Natural Waist	17½	12¾	Shoulder Measure (front)	14
40	Full Length	40	14¾	2d " " "	16
7¼	Width of Back	7¾	17½	Slope of Shoulder	18¾
21	to Elbow	21½	9	Small of Waist	10
31	Full Length of Sleeve	32	9½	Hip Measure	10½
12¾	Blade Measure	13¾	39	Breast Measure	39
			36	Waist Measure	36

TO DRAFT.

SQUARE lines A5 and AB. From A to 2 is front measure taken from 8 to B, with 1 inch added. 2 to 1 is depth of scye on back, with ¾ inch added. From 1 to 3 is natural waist; to 5, full length; 6 is half way between 1 and 2. Square lines 1, 6, 2, 3, 4 and 5. Go in an inch at 3 and 5. Draw line from 1 to 3 and from 3 to 5. From 1 to 7 is ⅛ breast measure and ⅜ of an inch added. Go up ¾ inch. From 6 to 17 is width of back. Add ½ inch. Draw line from 17, up and down, to bottom of coat. Go up from 17 1½ inches for shoulder line. Take out ¾ inch from back at 23. Shape back, and hollow ½ inch at 3 in center back. From 2 to 8 is blade measure. From 8 to 3 is ecliptic measure. Whatever the difference from 8 to 3, take out same amount on ecliptic line between back and forepart. Measure size of back at 3, placing the amount at 10, and measure back to 13. Measure back at 4, placing the amount at 11; measure back to 14; add 1 inch to these two measures at 13 and 14. Draw a line from 13 through 14 for spring of coat. Now shape side of forepart according to the ecliptic measure through 20, and take out, under the arm, the difference between small of waist and ecliptic measure. Divide the width of shoulder of back by 3, and place ⅓ in front of 8 at 20. Square up from 20 to 15. On line 20 go down from 15 ⅛ breast measure. Measure back from B to 16 half collar measure plus ¼ inch. From 2 to 9 is half breast measure. Measure size of back at 3 and place the amount at 13, and measure out half waist measure to 12. From 9 at breast to front of coat is 6 inches for double-breasted, and from 9 to front 4½ inch in fly front. From 12 to front in a double-breasted, add 5½ inches; in a fly front, add from 12 to front 4 inches. Now measure from 6 to 21 on back, and place the amount at 8, and measure up to 22 the height of center of shoulder. Now cut out back and place 15 and 7 together and 21 and 22. Shape shoulder as represented. Shape arm-hole. Take out ½ inch between back and top of forepart on side. Shape as represented on diagram.

KNIGHTS TEMPLAR Coats are cut the same as a single-breasted frock coat, with the exceptions of a half inch smaller on breast and waist with a full skirt. Made with side edges in the back pleats, and also with a standing collar 1½ inches in back and 1¼ inches in front at neck. Nine ball buttons on front divided equally from collar to waist seam. Two buttons on top of hip and two buttons on bottom of side edges. For double-breasted for Eminent and Past Eminent Commanders, add the lapels extra, with 9 buttons on each side of breast.

A MILITARY BLOUSE is cut the same as a single-breasted sack, with only 3 inches added to breast and waist, instead of 3½ inches as sack.

THE CASSOCK is cut tight-fitting in body, with a very full skirt with 3 large box pleats—one box pleat in center of back and one on each side of hip. Cut to waist, same as frock coat. Back at waist is 3 inches wide, and from waist down same as a ladies' ulster. The front is closed with from 38 to 40 buttons of vest size. The Cassock should be long enough to reach to within 3 inches of the heel of shoe. Standing collar.

THE CLERICAL FROCK is cut the same as a Knight Templar coat, with the omission of side edges in back, and only 6 buttons on front, spaced evenly.

THE COACHMAN'S OVERCOAT is cut the same as a frock overcoat, with the lapels straight at top instead of slanting, and a turn-down collar, with side edges in back pleats, with 6 buttons on each side of breast and 3 on each side edge.

THE FOOTMAN'S FROCK is single-breasted, with 4 buttons on front and 3 on side edges in back pleats.

THE RAGLAN is a single-breasted overcoat, with sleeves running up to a point in the neck seam. It is very seldom worn in this country.

A COAT FOR HUNCHBACK is drafted the same as any coat. The actual measures place the extra goods in the place where it is most needed.

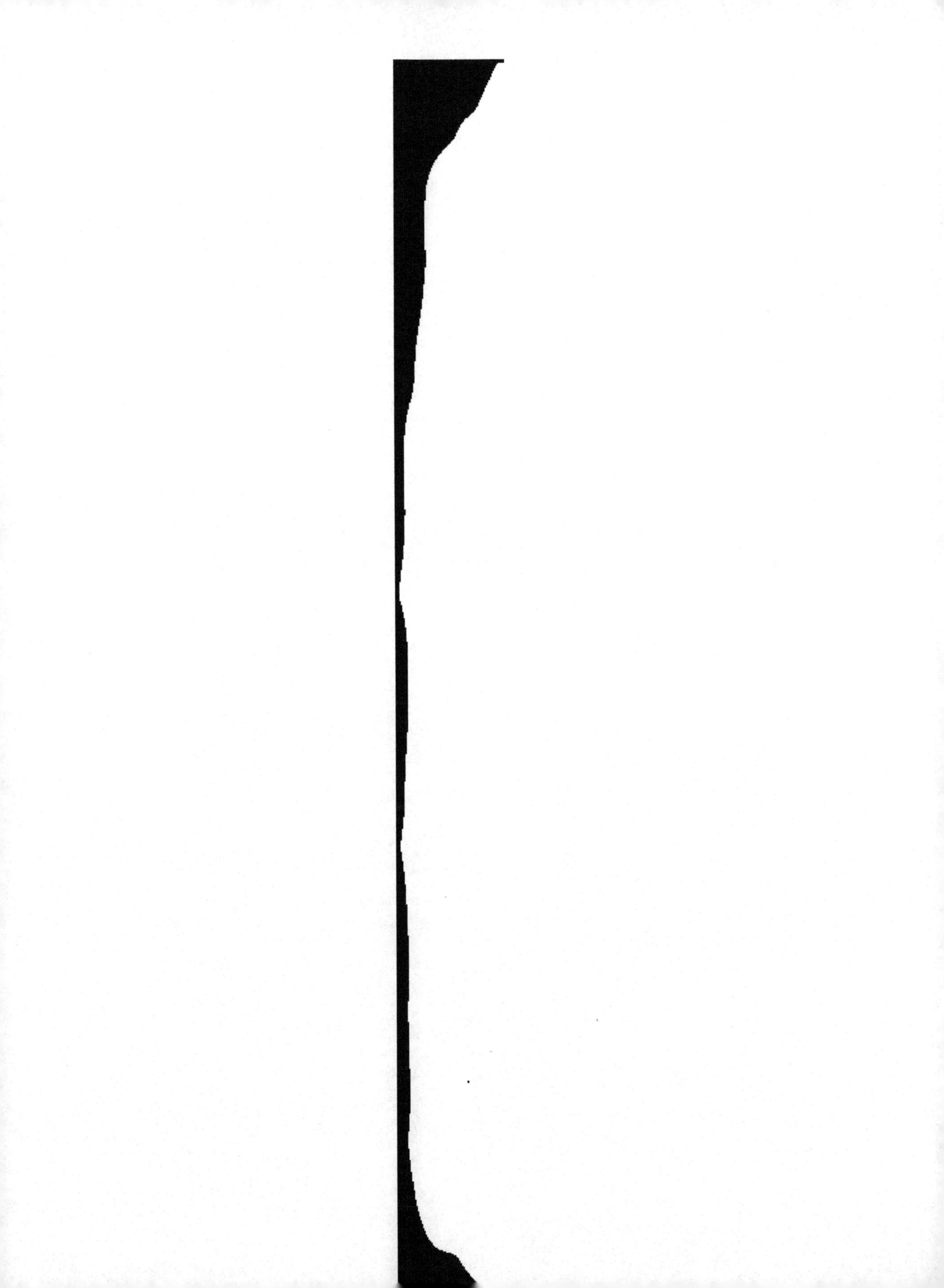

CPSIA information can be obtained
at www.ICGtesting.com
Printed in the USA
LVOW05s0333011017
550696LV00006B/1002/P